BEHOLD, HE COMETH

ARE YOU PREPARED?

ENOCH ADEJARE ADEBOYE

An imprint of Pneuma Life Publishing
Largo, MD

Copyright © 2002 Enoch Adejare Adeboye

Christian Living Books, Inc.
An imprint of Pneuma Life Publishing, Inc.
P. O. Box 7584
Largo, MD 20792
301-218-9092
www.christianlivingbooks.com

All rights reserved under the international copyright law. No part of this book may be reproduced or transmitted in any form or by any means, electronic or mechanical, including photocopying, recording, or by any information storage and retrieval system, without the express, written permission of the author or publisher.

ISBN 0-9711760-4-3

Printed in the United States of America

Unless otherwise markets, all Scripture quotations are taken from the *Holy Bible, New International Version* ®. NIV®. Copyright © 1973, 1978, 1984 by International Bible Society. Used by permission of Zondervan. All rights reserved.

CONTENTS

ONE   1
"BEHOLD, HE COMETH"

TWO   5
FOR THINE MAKER IS THINE HUSBAND

THREE   13
THE MARRIAGE OF THE LAMB

FOUR   21
JUDGMENT SEAT OF CHRIST

FIVE   29
A BRIDE WITHOUT SPOTS, WRINKLES OR BLEMISHES

SIX   39
YOU HAVE A CHOICE

PREFACE

We are already in the End Times that will ultimately climax in the end of the world. There is no more likely time to expect the return of Jesus Christ than now. Jesus, the bridegroom, is coming to take His bride away. This bride will be without spots, wrinkles or blemishes. There will be a marriage feast for the Bride and crowns will be distributed.

To qualify as Jesus' bride, you must be a born-again Christian and live a holy life. Anything short of that will quicken your flight to hell.

We believe that after reading this book, you will be able to make up your mind where you want to go—Heaven or hell. You have a choice between eternal joy and eternal pain. Of course, we prefer that you choose Heaven. It will be our joy to meet you there.

— Pastor E. A. Adeboye

CHAPTER ONE

"BEHOLD, HE COMETH"

Let's start by defining our terms of reference. "Behold" means "watch out," "pay attention" and "be alert." It is a warning, one that is often shouted.

"Behold, He cometh." Who is He? Of course, the answer is Jesus—the Lion of Judah, the King of kings, Lord of lords, the Great Judge, the I Am That I Am. He is Emmanuel, the Prince of Peace. If we were to ask Jesus, "Who is He that cometh?" he would give us a strange answer.

> *At midnight the cry rang out: "Here's the bridegroom! Come out to meet him!"* (Matthew 25:6)

Now there are all kinds of bridegrooms. They can be found anywhere. But the one who is coming is the

BEHOLD, HE COMETH

Bridegroom or, better still, *my* Bridegroom! Let's check two passages of Scripture.

> *No, we speak of God's wisdom, a wisdom that has been hidden and that God destined for our glory before time began.* (1 Corinthians 2:7-10)

> *None of the rulers of this age understood it, for if they had they would not have crucified the Lord of glory. However, as it is written: No eye has seen, no ear has heard, no mind has conceived what God has prepared for those who love him. But God has revealed it to us by his Spirit. The Spirit searches all things, even the deep things of God. Look he is coming with the clouds, and every eye will see him, even those who pierced him; and all the peoples of the earth will mourn because of him. So shall it be! Amen.* (Revelation 1:7)

There is a difference between coming with the clouds and coming in the clouds. Let us link these passages with I Thessalonians:

> *According to the Lord's own word, we tell you that we who are still alive, who are left till the coming of the Lord, will certainly not precede those who have fallen asleep. For the Lord himself will come down from heaven with a loud command with the voice of the archangel and with the trumpet call of God and the dead in Christ will rise first. After that, we who are still alive and are left will be caught up together with them in the clouds to meet the Lord in the air, and so we will be with the Lord forever.*
> (I Thessalonians 4:15-17)

"BEHOLD, HE COMETH"

We are made in the image of God, who said, "Let us make man in our image." So we, like God, have a triune or three-part nature. God gave man body, soul and spirit. The body is what we can see on the outside. Inside is the spirit, which is enveloped by the soul. When a man dies, the body, made of dust, will go back to the dust and the spirit enveloped by the soul will go to one of two places. If you are a born-again Christian, the moment you die and your body goes to the dust, your soul and spirit will go to a place called Paradise. If you are not born-again, you will go to a place that the Bible describes in the story of the rich man and Lazarus: a place of fire and unquenchable thirst. It's also referred to as a place of weeping and wailing and gnashing of teeth.

Paradise is not Heaven, just as Lagos is not Nigeria and Washington D.C. is not America. However, Paradise is *in* Heaven. You will remain in Paradise until the Lord returns to the Earth. When the Lord is ready to return, something will happen. This is unveiled in Revelations:

> *And I saw heaven standing open and there before me was a white horse: whose rider is called Faithful and True. With justice he judges and makes war. His eyes are like blazing fire, and on his head are many crowns. He has a name written on him that no one knows but he himself. He is dressed in a robe dipped in blood and his name is The Word of God. The armies of heaven were following him, riding on white horses and dressed in fine linen, white and clean.* (Revelation 19:11-14)

If you pass on from this world before the Lord returns, you will be part of that army. You will be dressed in white, on your own white horse. Christ, the Captain, will be in front with the entire army of Heaven in tow. The perspective from the earth will be of the Captain leading millions of people dressed in white, riding white horses, in a scene that would look like moving clouds. This is what the Bible describes as *"He is coming with the clouds."*

Once in the air, the Lord will wait and His armies will be dispatched to the earth, to pick up the bodies of saints who had slept in the Lord from their graves. Meanwhile, those of us who are alive and well will not even know what is happening. When the dead pick up their bodies, they will become complete again—body, soul and spirit. Then they will join Jesus Christ in the air. For those of us who remain, our bodies will also change and we will meet Jesus Christ in the air.

CHAPTER TWO

FOR THINE MAKER IS THINE HUSBAND

Before human history began, somewhere in the distant past, the Trinity-in-Council held a meeting. God the Father was the Chairman. The Legal Adviser that day was God the Son.

> *And he will be called Wonderful Counselor, Mighty God, Everlasting Father, Prince of Peace.*
> (Isaiah 9:6)

The advice He gave is recorded in Genesis:

> *Let us make man in our image. (Genesis 1:26)*

Those were the very first lines in the history book of the human race. Man was made in the image of God Almighty.

BEHOLD, HE COMETH

You may want to ask some questions like, "Why were we created at all? Why are we here on earth? What exactly are we doing here? Why did God bother to create us?" The simple answer is, God wants to be married. (Isaiah 54:5)

God the Father decided to choose a wife for Himself among men and He chose the nation Israel. He even paid a bride price.

> *But now, this is what the Lord says—he who formed you, O Jacob, he who formed you; O Israel; Fear not, for I have redeemed you; I have summoned you by name; you are mine. When you pass through the waters, I will be with you and when you pass through the rivers, they will not sweep over you. When you walk through the fire, you will not be burned; the flames will not set you ablaze. For I am the Lord, your God, the Holy One of Israel, your Savior. I give Egypt for your ransom, Cush and Seba in your stead. Since you are precious and honored in my sight and because I love you, I will give men in exchange for your life.*
> (Isaiah 43:1-4)

God paid a price. Why is it that God drowned the army of Egypt in the Red Sea? He was paying a bride price for Israel. Why did He kill all the first-born in Egypt? Part of the bride price. The destruction of Syria and Seba? Also part of the bride price. And each time Israel offended God, the Bible stated that Israel was a whore.

At that meeting of the Trinity-in-Council, it was also decided that God the Son would select His own wife from all the nations of the world. Not just Israel, but from all the nations. When we get to Heaven, we are going to meet with those people who make up the bride of Christ. The Bible tells us in Revelations:

> *After this I looked and there before me was a great multitude, that no one could count, from every nation, tribe, people and language, standing before the throne and in front of the Lamb. They were wearing white robes and were holding palm branches in their hands. And they cried out in a loud voice; "Salvation belongs to our God, who sits on the throne and to the Lamb."*
> (Revelation 7:9-10)

It was agreed that Jesus Christ would marry. He would pick people from every tribe, every tongue, and every nation. It was also agreed that anyone who would be the bride of Christ must be approved by God the Father. Jesus Christ confirms this:

> *No one can come to me unless the Father who sent me draws him and I will raise him up on the last day.* (John 6:44)

The Trinity-in-Council agreed that if God the Father were to pay a bride price, then God the Son must also pay a bride price—with His own blood. This was why He came.

> *You know it was not with perishable things such as silver or gold that you were redeemed from the empty way of life handed down to you from your forefathers. But with the precious blood of Christ, a Lamb without blemish or defect. He was chosen*

BEHOLD, HE COMETH

before the creation of the world but was revealed in these last times for your sake. (I Peter 1:18-20)

Do you not know that your body is the temple of the Holy Spirit, who is in you, whom you have received from God? You are not your own.

You were bought at a price. Therefore honor God with your body. (I Corinthians 6:19-20)

So when Jesus came here the first time He came to be introduced to His bride and to pay the bride price. The Bible tells us:

How God anointed Jesus of Nazareth with the Holy Spirit and power and how he went around doing good and healing all who were under the power of the devil because God was with him. (Acts 10:38)

This was His way of introducing Himself. When He comes the second time, He will be coming for the full marriage ceremony and consummation.

We human beings have our own calendar. We talk of months, weeks and days. God has His own calendar, too, which is a bit different from ours. The Bible tells us that a day in God's calendar is the equivalent of one thousand years in our calendar. So when Jesus Christ came the first time, there began, in the calendar of God, what we now call the End Times or the Last Days.

FOR **THINE MAKER IS THINE HUSBAND**

The End Times consist of three days in God's calendar. One is called the Present Day, which started from the day Jesus Christ ascended into Heaven and when the Holy Spirit fell on the Apostles. This day has not yet ended. Next will come the Day of Jesus Christ, and this will be approximately one thousand years. This is the millennium. Then will come the third day, which is the Day of God—the "Forever" day. Another name for it is Eternity. It is that day when there will be no night.

All three days are crucial. Let's take a closer look at the Present Day. After Jesus Christ had introduced Himself to His bride and paid the bride price, He went home. He sent the Holy Spirit to act as a go-between and to glorify Jesus as He got busy in Heaven preparing the perfect mansions for His bride. The Holy Spirit keeps Jesus Christ keenly on our minds so that we never forget Him—something typical of an earthly go-between in a matchmaking for marriage. If you are wise, as soon as you have given your life to Jesus Christ as your Lord and Savior, as soon as you are married to Jesus Christ, if you want to ask anything from Him, you had better ask the go-between, the Holy Spirit. The Bible tells us that we do not know how to pray as we ought to, but the Holy Spirit helps us.

Let's apply this analogy. Any time you want something from your husband Jesus Christ, send the go-between. The Holy Spirit will go to Jesus Christ and say something like this: "Do you know that every girl is thinking of buying something beautiful for Christmas? The only one who has no money to shop is your wife, and I have already told her that you are the greatest, the richest, that the earth is yours and everything in it." (Psalm 24:1) Jesus Christ is going to say, "Tell me what the others are buying." The Holy Spirit will reply, "They have been buying gowns, hats and bags to match." Jesus Christ will ask, "How many do you think I should buy for my wife?" The Holy Spirit will reply, "Well, because of what I have said about you, maybe half a dozen will be all right." And the dialogue goes on and on.

The Holy Spirit, right now, is branding the brides of Jesus Christ. He comes to you and whispers to you to give your life to the Lord. He tells you Jesus Christ is wonderful and kind, and that He can do all things. The moment you say "Yes," He puts a mark on you. That's the seal the Bible talks about in Ephesians 1:13. This is a mark that every opposing power is able to see very clearly. You may not see it but demons can. This is why the Bible says we are more than conquerors.

Meanwhile, Jesus Christ is in Heaven preparing for His wedding. He is preparing the wedding chamber.

> *Do not let your hearts be troubled, Trust in God, trust also in me. In my Father's house are many rooms; if it were not so, I would have told you. I am going there to prepare a place for you. And if I go and prepare a place for you, I will come back and take you to be with me that you also may be where I am.* (John 14:1-3)

If there are many rooms or mansions in Heaven, why does He have to go and prepare a place? There will be no admission without reservations because there will be too many people. So He has to go and reserve a place for you. If He has not, it is probably because you have not given your life to Him.

He says that when He has finished the preparation, He will come back again for us. Why must the bridegroom

FOR **THINE MAKER IS THINE HUSBAND**

Himself come back for us? Why can't He send Gabriel or Michael or any of the other angels? Why must He come Himself? The Bible tells us that God dwells in a glory that no man can approach. There are categories of angels. There are angels and there are angels. There are angels that stand in the presence of God. However, they are not very close to the presence of God. They dare not get very close. The glory of God will wipe them out in a jiffy if they get too close.

There was a man of God that has now gone to be with the Lord. He said that God gave him a glimpse of what the throne-room setting is like. The nearest any angel can get to God is about one thousand miles. Even at that distance, he has to cover his face with his two wings or else his eyes will be blinded by the blazing radiance of God. If Jesus Christ were to send an angel to bring you, he would take you as far as one thousand miles from God and leave you. This is why Jesus Christ has to come Himself. Another reason is that certain doors into Heaven—the everlasting doors—do not open to anybody except Jesus Christ. David refers to this in Psalms:

> *Yet I am always with you; you hold me by my right hand. You guide me with your counsel and afterward you will take into glory.* (Psalm 73:23-24)

If you die here on earth and Jesus is not standing by your side to hold your hand and lead you home, I assure you—you are going to hell. But if you are one of His before you leave here, He will come and stand by your side, and you will just sail through the valley of the shadow of death. When you get to the everlasting doors, the King of glory will go in, holding you by the right hand and, of course, no angel can stop you. Where He is, you will always be.

The moment you understand that Jesus Christ is your Husband, and the moment it becomes clear to you that you are His wife, the question of sanctification becomes easy. A sanctified person is just a favorite wife. If I am the favorite wife of the King, or the wife of the President, I cannot imagine indulging in adultery. It's unthinkable. How can I be the wife of the President and engage in any unbecoming acts in public, or even in private? The moment you know who you are, how you behave will fall into place accordingly.

Only God the Father knows the number of the brides of Jesus Christ. When this number is complete, there will be a trumpet call. But this is not an ordinary instrument; it is the trumpet of God. If you want to know how big the trumpet of God is, then you need to imagine how big the hands of God must be. If you want to know how big the hands of God are, you can start by checking out how big His legs are. The Bible tells us that when God wants to put his feet up, He uses the whole earth as His footstool. This will give you a rough idea of how big His hands must be. If He touches a mountain with His fingers, the mountain melts. So the trumpet of God is awesome; it is not a trivial thing. It is the trumpet an ordinary angel cannot blow, and angels are strong.

The cherubims are supposed to be super strong. In fact, the Bible says one of the cherubims can carry God as a horse will carry a man. One of His archangels will blow the trumpet because it must be heard all over the universe when it sounds. I wish it would sound today, so that we can be gone. But because some people are not yet ready to go, maybe we should wait a little while longer.

CHAPTER THREE

THE MARRIAGE OF THE LAMB

When the trumpet of God sounds, it is to announce to everybody that the table is set, all the preparations are complete and the wedding can start. You must have read about it in Revelations:

> *Then a voice came from the throne, saying: "Praise our God, all you his servants, you who fear him, both small and great!" Then I heard what sounded like a great multitude, like the roar of rushing waters and like loud peals of thunder, shouting: "Hallelujah! For our Lord God Almighty reigns. Let us rejoice and be glad and give him glory! For the wedding of the Lamb has come, and his bride has made herself ready. Fine linen, bright and clean, was given her to wear."* [Fine linen stands for the

righteous acts of the saints.] *Then the angel said to me, "Write: Blessed are those who are invited to the wedding supper of the Lamb!" And he added, "These are the true words of God."*

(Revelation 19:5-9)

As soon as the trumpet sounds, the Lord takes over from Heaven and the transformation takes place. We will all meet in the air. The next thing Jesus Christ will do is to present us to His Father. God the Father is going to conduct a wedding some day soon, one that will join the heavens to the earth. It is going to be the biggest of all nuptials and the pastor on that day will be God the Father. The bridegroom is Jesus Christ and I am the bride. John the Baptist will be the best man and Ruth the chief bridesmaid.

At the wedding, there is going to be an orchestra of 144,000 men that will render two special numbers. One will be composed by Moses. Jesus Christ Himself will compose the other. The Bible states in Revelations:

And sang the song of Moses the servant of God and the song of the Lamb: "Great and marvelous are your deeds, Lord God Almighty. Just and true are your ways, King of the ages." (Revelation 15:3)

The wedding is going to take place in the air because, right now, the air is the headquarters of our enemies. God wants to fulfill the prophecy of David: *"You prepare a table before me in the presence of my enemies. You anoint my head with oil; my cup overflows."*

The wedding of Jesus Christ was so crucial to Him that on His last night on earth, He prayed a fantastic prayer

THE MARRIAGE OF THE LAMB

recorded in John 17. Jesus Christ asked for two things. One was that the Father should glorify Him with the same glory He had before the world began. His second prayer was that the Father should look after Jesus' bride till He returns. This shows you how important you are to Jesus Christ. This is why I am sure that it does not matter how hard the devil may try, he will not succeed in our lives because the Father is looking after us.

On the wedding day, we are going to be so happy, so joyous, that we will cry. Some people say there will be no crying in Heaven, but they did not read their Bible very well. There will be cries of joy. The Bible tells us that when we begin to cry for joy, God will take His handkerchief and He will wipe away all tears from our eyes. Then the party will begin. It is going to last for seven solid years. What we will eat during the party will include the fruits of the Tree of Life and we will drink from the River of Life.

The Bible tells us that those who are invited to the wedding are blessed people. Some people say, "I wish I would be invited," but they've got it wrong. If you are invited, you are a guest, not Christ's bride. Nobody invites a bride to her own wedding! We are the ones who will be getting married. And we are going to invite Abraham, Isaac, Jacob, Elijah, Elisha and David.

After the marriage ceremony and seven years of conjugal bliss, we will be coming back here for one thousand years. Why? I asked God this question some time ago. The Lord explained that, even though our bodies would have been transformed, we have been so conditioned to suffering on earth that we will need one thousand years to be re-oriented. We have been so traumatized by life's adversities here that, if we were allowed to go straight to

BEHOLD, HE COMETH

Heaven with our earthly mentality, the joy in Heaven would destroy us. God says you need a thousand years to gradually "rev up" your joy before you can really qualify for the heights of happiness in Heaven. I am looking forward to that day. I pray I see you there.

Another reason for the thousand-year reign of King Jesus on earth is that our Husband, the Bridegroom, wants to spend His honeymoon in the very land where He paid the bride price. One thousand years of honeymoon! Glory be to God forever!

Those who are not of Christ will also need those thousand years to get used to suffering before they go to the Lake of Fire. Hell was initially custom-made for the devil and his angels, not for human beings. The punishment is so severe that human beings cannot go there directly. They have to gradually adjust to suffering on an increasing basis until they meet the devil in the Lake of Fire. I pray you will not be one of those hell-bound.

The real purpose of creation is for God to get married. I want you to know that every time somebody gives their life to Jesus Christ, what they are saying is that they accept Jesus Christ as their husband. Salvation is exactly like a marriage contract. When you get married to Jesus Christ, three things change. First, there will be a change of name. You now become a child of God. That is one reason why Muslims think we are peculiar people. Only born-again Christians dare call themselves children of God.

THE **MARRIAGE** OF THE **LAMB**

There will also be a change of address. Whether you know it or not, the day you get married to Jesus Christ, according to the Bible, you are transferred from the kingdom of darkness to the Kingdom of God's dear Son. You used to live with the devil in darkness, in sickness, in poverty. But the day you say you are married to Jesus, you change your spiritual address. The Bible says that, even now, we are seated with Jesus in the heavenly places.

And lastly, there is a change of responsibilities. When you were not yet married, you were free to do whatever you liked. However, from the day you are married to Jesus Christ, God's words become law.

Therefore, when you say you surrender to Jesus, you are asking for a change of name, a change of address and a change of responsibilities. You've probably heard the testimonies of people who insist they have had no need to see doctors since they gave their lives to Jesus Christ. This is true—you should not have to seek help from physicians when you're married to the Great Physician.

God bless doctors. I love them and I thank God for the difference they made in my life before I came to Christ in 1977. That was the year they last saw me in their hospitals, and they will never see me again. However, if not for the skills God gave them to drill several holes in my body and pump injections in, I probably would have died before I met Jesus Christ.

The moment you are married to Him, He will look after your health. If you have given your life to Jesus Christ and you are still sickly then you must re-examine your commitment to Him. Ask me and I will tell you that He is the Great Physician. He has never failed and He will

BEHOLD, HE COMETH

heal you. When you marry the right man, all your burdens become his. This is what the Bible means when it states:

> *And my God will meet all your needs according to his glorious riches in Christ Jesus.*
> (Philippians 4:19)

Jesus is the Bridegroom. He will satisfy all your needs the moment you become a believer.

The satisfaction waiting for us in Heaven is so great that Jesus gave some suggestions on how to avoid stumbling blocks to that goal.

> *And if your right hand causes you to sin, cut it off and throw it away. It is better for you to lose one part of your body than for your whole body to go into hell.* (Matthew 5:30)

When I was a new believer, I often asked why God would tell me to cut my right hand off if He really loves me. God's answer came to me in a vision.

In that vision, I saw lots of Christians singing joyfully and strolling on the highway to Heaven. Suddenly I saw a man advancing from far behind, running, pushing and shoving. I wondered, "Is this a Christian?" This Scripture flashed into my mind:

> *From the days of John the Baptist until now, the kingdom of heaven has been forcefully advancing, and forceful men lay hold of it.* (Matthew 11:12)

THE **MARRIAGE** OF THE **LAMB**

But as I was meditating on this, I suddenly realized why this man was in a hurry. The gates of Heaven, which actually appeared to me as one huge sliding door, were about to close. By the time he got there, the gap in the door was too narrow for him to go in face first, so he had to squeeze through sideways. As he did, the gate finally shut and his right hand was left outside. Then the angel said to him, "Sir, the instructions are that nothing more can come in. So that I can shut this gate properly, will you go out or do we cut off your right hand?" This is the question I have for Christians today: If you were that man, what would be your answer?

Not all born-again Christians will get to Heaven. If we are ever going to get there, our dedication will have to be far greater than it is at the moment. We must examine our lives closely and think of all those things that could prevent us from entering Heaven. Let us ask the Almighty to cut them off. If you are not able to let go gently, tell Him to remove by force anything that will not allow you to enter into glory.

CHAPTER FOUR

JUDGMENT SEAT OF CHRIST

Before the millennium starts—that is, after we have been in the air with Jesus Christ for seven years—the Bridegroom will summon all of us to His judgment seat for decoration.

> *For we must all appear before the judgment seat of Christ, that each one may receive what is due him for the things done while in the body whether good or bad.* (2 Corinthians 5:10)

Meanwhile, every bride is already wearing a beautiful bridal gown as recorded in Revelation 19:8. It is made of linen, white and clean. It is written in Timothy **that** we will also wear crowns:

> *I have fought the good fight, I have finished the race, I have kept the faith. Now there is in store for*

BEHOLD, HE COMETH

> *me the crown of righteousness which the Lord the righteous Judge will award to me on that day and not only to me but also to all who have longed for his appearing.* (2 Timothy 4:7-8)

We will get that crown, but before our decoration comes our individual debriefing where the works of every man and woman will be judged. One by one, we will be summoned and an angel will bring a huge package of all our words, thoughts and deeds, from the day we were born-again until the day Jesus Christ returned. Everything we did before we were born-again is already forgotten; the blood of Jesus cleansed us from all prior sins. The angel will throw the package into a fire that burns close by.

> *If it is burned up, he will suffer loss; he himself will be saved but only as one escaping through the flames.* (I Corinthians 3:15)

If your package contains nothing that is of eternal value, you will watch as it burns away completely. If the contents are considered to be of eternal value, the package will burn off but the contents will remain solid.

> *Since then, we know what it is to fear the Lord we try to persuade men. What we are is plain to God and I hope it is also plain to your conscience.*
> (2 Corinthians 5:11)

You will watch in terror as the fire of God tests your works. You will also get to see the testing of the works of famous evangelists and people who are called mighty men of God. You may see many lifetime packages reduced to rubble. And when it is your turn, you will

JUDGMENT SEAT OF CHRIST

definitely feel some beads of sweat on your brow since you cannot tell what will endure.

After the fire has consumed all that is consumable, rewards will follow. According to the word of God, rewards will be given not only for the good works that you have done but also for the bad ones. In other words, your "credits" will be reconciled against your "debits." It is the balance that will be rewarded.

Also taken into consideration will be those things you failed to do. These include opportunities that you had to serve the Lord that you ignored or neglected.

> *Anyone then who knows the good he ought to do and doesn't do it, sins.* (James 4:17)

It is not only what we achieved that will be rewarded. What we should have achieved will also be taken into consideration, and the reward will be commensurate.

Also under consideration will be all the words you have spoken from the day you were born-again until the day Jesus Christ returns—all the words you spoke on behalf of Jesus, to testify for Him, to glorify Him or to worship Him. The words you spoke in gossip, in backbiting or in lewd jokes will also be taken into account.

> *But I tell you men will have to give account on the day of judgment for every careless word they have spoken. For by your words you will be acquitted and by your words you will be condemned.*
> (Matthew 12:36-37)

Even your thoughts will be tested:

BEHOLD, HE COMETH

> *Therefore judge nothing before the appointed time; wait till the Lord comes. He will bring to light what is hidden in darkness and will expose the motives of men's hearts. At that time each will receive his praise from God.* (I Corinthians 4:5)

After these evaluations end, some people will be decorated for all the enduring good they did. Some will receive more crowns and, in addition, some will receive the Crown of Life. Remember, we all have on the Crown of Righteousness.

> *Do not be afraid of what you are about to suffer, I tell you the devil will put some of you in prison to test you and you will suffer persecution for ten days. Be faithful even to the point of death and I will give you the Crown of Life.* (Revelations 2:10)

Some people will receive the Crown of Rejoicing, which is given to those who love winning souls.

> *For what is our hope, our joy or the crown in which we will glory in the presence of our Lord Jesus when he comes?* (I Thessalonians 2:19)

> *Therefore my brothers, you whom I love and long for, my joy and crown that is how you should stand firm in the Lord, dear friends!* (Philippians 4:1)

Others will receive the Crown of Glory. This belongs to those of us who are elders, pastors and chapter presidents: those who led others in the way of God.

And some will get all these crowns plus stars to embellish them. I am convinced that the number of souls you win will determine the number of stars on your crowns.

JUDGMENT SEAT OF CHRIST

Those who are wise will shine like the brightness of the heavens and those who lead many to righteousness, like the stars for ever and ever. (Daniel 12:3)

If you end up in Heaven without having won a single soul for Jesus Christ, you will receive your Crown of Righteousness but it will have no stars. If you win one soul, then you've earned one star. I wonder how some of us will be able to carry all our stars because there will be so many! I have seen brethren winning a hundred souls every day, and for each one there will be a star. However, there is a condition to be met: It is not the souls that you win that determine the stars, but the souls you win that actually make it to heaven. If you win souls who backslide before Jesus Christ comes, you suffer a loss. This means we have to be more dedicated about our follow-ups, since it is not enough to win souls. We must make sure that these souls—our fruits—remain in Christ. I pray that there will be many stars on your crown, in Jesus' name.

Regardless of the number of stars in your crown, everybody will weep when that day comes because you will discover that you have not done enough. I remember a few years ago when I spent some time with the Almighty God alone at the Redemption Camp. I was singing, dancing in the moonlight and having fellowship with the Almighty God. Then around 4 a.m. God began to speak to me, asking me questions. At that time, I thanked Him because I thought that I was doing mighty things for the Lord. But by the time He finished asking about twenty questions, I knew I had done nothing. By His standards, I scored precious little.

BEHOLD, HE COMETH

When you get to Heaven, you will see the reward for the little you have done. But when you imagine the reward that could have been yours, had you only done what He expected you to do, you will weep. However, God will wipe all tears from our eyes.

And then there are those people whose works will be completely consumed by fire. They will go back to their seats decorated with shame:

> *And now dear Brethren continue in Him so that when He appears we may be confident and unashamed before Him at His coming.* (I John 2:28)

I pray that on that day you will not be put to shame. If you stand before the Lord of Lords and see other people getting many stars, you may think, "But I won them to Christ." You may be left wondering why your work did not make it through the fire. If everything burns, how shameful it will be! But at least you are already in Heaven. On that day many of us will see the stars of others and feel empty. However, over there you will not feel envious.

The disclosure of our true motives may cause many of our achievements to burn. Some people give to the Gospel because they want to be seen. I can assure you that everything you do for appearances is going to be burnt on that day. Some work for God because they want to be known. Any work done with that kind of motive will burn to cinders.

The Almighty God taught me a lesson along this line some years ago. He wanted to know why I was working so hard to win many souls. My reason was based on acquiring many stars. He told me that I had it all wrong.

JUDGMENT SEAT OF CHRIST

He said the reason I should work hard for Him is because I love Him. Period!

Do not give to God because you want a reward—although the reward will come, no doubt about that. Give offerings because you love Jesus. Do godly things because you love God. Somebody once asked why anyone would sing a song that calls Jesus "Darling". I told him that Jesus is more than a darling, he is the love of my life and my life itself. Is Jesus Christ your love too? If He is your love, your life will change. Many of us do good works simply because of our love for Him. That's the way it should be.

CHAPTER FIVE

A BRIDE WITHOUT SPOTS, WRINKLES OR BLEMISHES

The Bible says Jesus Christ is coming back for a bride without spots, without wrinkles and without blemishes.

> *Husbands, love your wives, just as Christ loved the church and gave himself up for her to make her holy, cleansing her by the washing with water through the word, and to present her to himself as a radiant church, without stain or wrinkle or any other blemish, but holy and blameless.*
>
> (Ephesians 5:25-27)

Only those believers who meet Jesus Christ's strict conditions will become his bride. But will every believer go to Heaven? The answer is yes and no. I will explain. Some born-again Christians who satisfy the conditions we are about to examine will go during Rapture, during

BEHOLD, HE COMETH

the period the Bible calls the First Resurrection. Those are the ones who will be married to Jesus Christ. However, I assure you that there will be a lot of born-again Christians left behind. On the Sunday after the return of Jesus Christ, after He has taken His bride, the Church will still be full. There will be pastors left behind to preach and evangelists to conduct crusades.

Those left behind will have to take a stand so they can qualify the second time. They must resist the mark and pressure of the anti-Christ, which will not be easy to do. They will finally end up in Heaven but they will not be part of the bride. The Bible calls them the tribulation saints. Those who will go at the Rapture—that is, those who will go the first time—must satisfy the following conditions:

1. They must be born-again Christians.
2. They must live a holy life.
3. They must be without blemish, spots and wrinkles.

The conditions have to be stringent. Jesus Christ is perfectly holy. He is the head, and the head is about to be joined to the body. If there is going to be a perfect union, the body must be as perfectly holy as the head. That is what Jesus Christ meant when He said:

> *Be perfect, therefore, as your heavenly Father is perfect.* (Matthew 5:48)

He did not say that you should be perfect as your pastor or your neighbor but your Father God, who is the epitome of perfection. The standard that will be used to determine who will marry Jesus is not set by any Church

A BRIDE WITHOUT SPOTS, WRINKLES OR BLEMISHES

denomination but by God himself. It is extremely high, much higher than what we have in Christendom today. I trust the Almighty God that, by the time He comes, some of us would have reached that standard. I pray you will be one of them.

What does He mean by "no blemishes"? Revelations gives us a list of those who will not make it:

> *But the cowardly, the unbelieving, the vile, the murderers, the sexually immoral, those who practice magic arts, the idolaters and all liars—their place will be in the fiery lake of burning sulfur. This is the second death.* (Revelations 21:8)

Demon possession must also be listed among the blemishes. If there remains a single demon in you, Jesus cannot marry you. That is understandable! There cannot be two captains in the same ship. Either you are for Jesus Christ or you are for the devil. If you know that there is a demon hiding in you, you must seek deliverance.

Let me assure you, nobody drinking alcohol in any form whatsoever is going with Jesus. In Revelations, God has made us royal:

> *And has made us to be a kingdom and priests to serve his God and Father—to him be glory and power for ever and ever! Amen.* (Revelation1:6)

> *It is not for kings, O Lemuel—not for kings to drink wine, not for rulers to crave beer.*
> (Proverbs 31:4)

According to the word of God, these are the only people allowed to drink as much alcohol as they like:

BEHOLD, HE COMETH

Give beer to those who are perishing, wine to those who are in anguish; let them drink and forget their poverty and remember their misery no more.
(Proverbs 31:6-7)

Those who want to go to hell are free to drink as much as they like; at least they will not know what is happening until they get to the flames.

Anyone who is not fully paying his or her tithes is not going either. Some people teach that if you do not pay your tithes, God will not bless you. This is true, but it's even more serious than that. You do not pay your tithes, you do not go to Heaven. Why? Heaven will harbor no robbers. The Bible calls those who do not pay their tithes robbers (Malachi 3:8).

What does He mean by "no spots"? One example is "white lies." This includes exaggerations like, "We held a seminar in our chapter and thousands came," when in fact the hall can only seat five hundred. You hear some evangelists say, "We conducted a crusade at the National Stadium in Lagos; one million people were there." No stadium anywhere in the world can take one million people. You may think that little white lies do not matter to Him. But it matters because His name is THE TRUTH and He is not going to be married to liars.

Years ago, when my father in the Lord (the founder of the Redeemed Christian Church of God, RCCG) was alive, I traveled to my town in southwestern Nigeria. When I came back, I realized I had forgotten to buy him something. I wanted to visit him but I could not imagine going to a man of God empty-handed. So I bought some oranges by the roadside and presented these to him as if I had brought them back from my trip. He asked if I had

A BRIDE WITHOUT SPOTS, WRINKLES OR BLEMISHES

bought the oranges by the roadside. The question came so suddenly that the answer I gave was yes. As soon as I said yes, the Holy Spirit told me that I had lied. I wondered, "What lie?" The Holy Spirit explained that the Man of God wanted know whether I bought the oranges between my hometown and Lagos. I asked what difference it made where I had bought them; after all, it did not affect the sweetness of the orange. The Holy Spirit said that I had told a lie and I should make amends. I obeyed and told Papa the truth. He looked at me, smiled and said, "Holy Spirit." He understood.

On my return trip from the United States via London some years back, I was asked at the Lagos airport to fill out customs forms declaring how much money I had. I did not bother to check the coins, only the notes, and I wrote down the amount. As the customs officer was about to stamp my form, he asked to see all the money I had. Before he was through with the question I began to imagine newspaper headlines: "Pastor caught at airport over currency deal!" Suddenly fear gripped my heart. I had coins that could add up to a lot of money. The officer saw that I was troubled. I told him my declaration was not correct and he gave me a new form to fill out. This time I counted all the coins and wrote the correct amount. When I finally got out of there, I said, "Lord, why did you do that to me?" The Lord replied, "Son, I cannot tolerate lies."

On another occasion, we were about to do some minor work at our campgrounds. I hired a surveyor to help out. We agreed on the size and cost of one long trench that needed to be dug, one hundred feet long. But when he took the measurements, he calculated one hundred meters instead. I noticed, and the Holy Spirit told me to correct him. I didn't. The man finished the measurements, I paid him the deposit and he turned to go. Suddenly one of the laborers hired to work on the site stretched his hand toward me for a handshake. For no apparent reason, he began to squeeze my hand and kept on squeezing. The pain was horrible. The thought flashed through my mind, "God, why?" The Holy Spirit said, "I cannot tolerate lies." I called the surveyor back and pointed out his mistake. Later, as l got in my car, God said to me, "I have chosen to marry you; I will not tolerate impurities." I wept like a baby, but I got the message. No spots means no spots.

Surprisingly, another spot is worry. There are many chronic worriers among Nigerian businessmen and women. They worry when they pitch for government contracts and when they win the contracts. They worry about the work to be done. And then they worry whether the government will pay them on time. Once they are paid, they worry about security.

> *Do not be anxious about anything, but in everything, by prayer and petition, with thanksgiving, present your requests to God.* (Philippians 4:6)

In modern language, that means you must never fret or worry. Here is a commandment from the bridegroom:

> *Do not let your hearts be troubled. Trust in God; trust also in me.* (John 14:1)

This means that the moment you begin to worry, you are saying, "I do not believe in God; I do not believe in Jesus." As long as you believe in and trust them, there is nothing to worry about.

A BRIDE WITHOUT SPOTS, WRINKLES OR BLEMISHES

When I became the general overseer of the Redeemed Christian Church of God in 1981, we had thirty-nine parishes. I really knew how to worry in those days and was always fretting about the churches. One day, as I was standing before the mirror in the bathroom, I saw that my hair was going gray. There is nothing wrong with gray hair, but at that time I was less than forty years old. So I asked God what was happening. He said that I was too worrisome. I replied that I was anxious because of His children. He said, "Are they *your* children?" I was able to stop worrying. And within a couple of weeks, all my hair regained its lustrous black sheen again.

Also in 1981, I visited a branch of our church in Ilorin, Western Nigeria. I was told of a woman who had confessed that she believed she had an appointment with death on the day she would become a mother. By this time she was already in labor at our Maternity Center. I tried to speak with the woman but she wouldn't respond. I told her that since she had already made it to the Maternity Center, she would not die. I prayed for her and left for Lagos. One hour later, she delivered her baby but the midwife discovered that there was another baby still in the womb. That was on Wednesday, but by the end of the day the other baby was yet to be born. Thursday and Friday passed and the second baby still did not come. To further complicate matters, the mother refused to see a specialist in a regular hospital. She believed that Jesus had brought the first baby to birth and He must also bring the second. On Saturday I received a delegation from Ilorin, concerned over the delayed birth of the twin. As a leader, I summoned up courage and told them that the baby would be born before they returned home.

BEHOLD, HE COMETH

As soon as they left, I ran upstairs to my prayer room and fell on my face before the Lord. I told Him I desperately needed help. God asked me why I didn't believe what I had told the Ilorin visitors. I said I believed but ... He said that if I believed there would be no "buts." Reports reached me later saying that before the delegation got back to church, *two* other babies were born. Since then my worries have disappeared.

Let's move on to "no wrinkles." What does that mean? The Lord gave me this analogy: Assume your wedding gown (your spiritual record) has been thoroughly cleansed and ironed and has no blemishes or spots. It is hanging on the wall, waiting for you to put it on and walk down the aisle of the Kingdom. Then just before the trumpet sounded, the wind blew a little, the gown fell and other garments dropped onto it. By the time it was retrieved from under the pile, there was a wrinkle all the way down. God says with that gown you will not qualify for the wedding.

I asked for explanations. Thank God, my Father speaks to me often. He explained in detail. For example, there is a popular but difficult passage in the Bible that states that if you are slapped on the right cheek, you must turn the left for another slap. You are not guilty of anything, but God demands that you invite another slap. He asked me if I would willingly obey this passage of Scripture. When I said I would run, He laughed. I don't know if anyone has ever heard God laugh, but He does. It is written in the Scriptures. When you are close to Him and talk with Him on an intimate basis, from time to time you will hear Him laugh.

He then gave an example: I was presented with keys to six houses, with a luxury car in each of six garages, on one condition. All these material goodies would be mine if I could successfully take a three-hour Greyhound bus trip without striving with anyone. But upon getting to the terminal some cranky fellow kicks me and then slaps me. God wanted to know what I would do. I said I would apologize to my assailant. God went on to ask what I would do if the fellow got irate and threatened to prevent me from getting on the bus. I replied that I would have to walk if I could not successfully find a Good Samaritan. In fact, I would even hide to avoid any more confrontations, just to get the six houses and six cars. God said, "If you can do that much for things that will perish, how much more will you be willing to do for the inestimable treasures of eternity?"

God shared something else about wrinkles with me. If you are ever going to make it to Heaven, you must learn to ignore both praise and criticism. If people criticize you, bless them. When they praise you, give glory to God. God will not share His glory with anybody. The moment they begin to praise you and you soak it in, you've missed the point.

A young king once decided to fight an older king. The old king prevailed but spared his life and to teach him a lesson, he gave him a glass of water, full to the brim. He told the young king, "My executioner will be behind you, holding his sword. Carry this cup of water down the long, winding street and back without spilling a drop. If you spill any, you will be killed immediately."

Meanwhile, the older king had arranged for people to wait on both sides of the road. Some cheered the young king on while others jeered at him. He began the journey knowing that his life was in that cup of water. Spill just a drop and he was dead. But he was able to carry it all the way without spilling a drop.

The old king then asked him which of the two groups had helped him the more. The younger man answered, "I did not know they were there. I was more concerned about not spilling a drop than any other thing." The Lord asked me, "You want to get there?" He said that I need to ignore those who praise me as well as the critics.

CHAPTER SIX

YOU HAVE A CHOICE

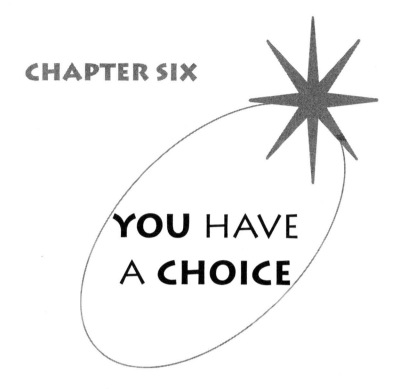

Not all Christians will go with Jesus at His return. There is no way all of us can go in the first round. As I have said, there will be two weddings. One will take place in the air, at the headquarters of our enemies. Our enemies will be kicked out so that we have time to enjoy ourselves. They will come and join their own son, the anti-Christ, on earth. At that time he will be conducting his own wedding; he will be married to the rest of the world.

If you do not go with us, you will have no problem with the anti-Christ—provided you receive his mark, his wedding ring. But you *will* have a problem with God Almighty! The Bible indicates that the main dish on the menu for the brides of the anti-Christ is something called pain, and tribulation of the highest order. The Bible reveals that at that time, people will invite death and

BEHOLD, HE COMETH

death will refuse to oblige them. I pray you will not be around at that time.

This means you have a choice. You have a choice of going in round one or waiting behind to slug it out with the anti-Christ. Take heart, you can still make it to Heaven later, if you succeed. The Bible states that it's possible, but it would be like passing through fire. At that time, you will pay for your salvation with your own blood.

You may not even be born-again and think I have been telling you fairy tales. We'll see about that. I want you to know that I have shared all this with you because I love you. Like I always tell people, if you find your friend in an air-conditioned room in a house that has caught fire and you need to alert him, disregard the "please do not disturb" notice on his door. If you leave him, the fire raging in other parts of his house will knock on his door and he may end up being a fire accident victim.

All unbelievers are living in a house that has already caught fire—the fire of hell. They can run out of the fire now and Jesus Christ will save their souls. To those already born-again, I challenge you to lay all those blemishes, spots and wrinkles in your life before the Almighty God. He will do something about them. It is those who conceal their sins who will not prosper. Those who confess and forsake them will enjoy the mercy of God. So if you say "Lord, I know that you know that I am a liar, a fornicator…" and you bare you soul to Him, you will be fully prepared because He will help you. When the Bridegroom comes, you will be ready to go with Him!

ABOUT THE AUTHOR

Enoch Adejare Adeboye became the General Overseer of The Redeemed Christian Church of God in 1981. The church has experienced unprecedented growth since he became its spiritual and administrative head. Under his leadership, the church hosts a monthly prayer vigil on the first Friday of every month at the headquarters in the Redemption Camp, on the outskirts of Lagos, Nigeria, attracting about 500,000 people per session. Similar meetings are held bi-annually in the United Kingdom and the United States, where the Church has a strong presence.

Also in the eighties, God led Pastor Adeboye to establish "model parishes" that continue to bring young people into the Kingdom in large numbers. The church now has over two million members in about four thousand parishes all over the world.

Pastor Adeboye, a mathematician who holds a Ph.D. in hydrodynamics, lectured at the University of Lagos, Nigeria for many years. He is also a prolific writer of many titles used by God to touch lives. He is married to Pastor Foluke Adeboye and they are blessed with four children.